DOING TIME

Papers from
Framingham Prison

Katherine A. Power

1.5

First Printing 2003
Second Printing 2010

Third Printing 2013

P.O. Box 1222
Taos, NM 87571
www.nighthawkpress.com

ISBN: 978-0615893778

"Sestina for Jaime" previously appeared in
The Best American Poetry 1996

Read and hear more of Katherine Power's work at
www.PracticalPeace.net

ANOTHER PLACE TO BE

A prison is a place under the sky, a particular spot on the planet, with its weather, its wild air and wild light. In the fortress-like pink stone building in downtown Boston, where I was jailed when I first surrendered, my cell looked down on a single city tree, six stories below. When I was moved to a cell that faced nothing but the slab walls and reflective windows of another wing of the jail, I sat at the wood platform that was bolted to the wall for a desk, looked out at the intense blank blue of the October sky and wondered how I would survive. At that moment, two Canada geese passed, their honking so loud I could hear it through the doubled panes of two-inch thick security glass. Then they were gone.

Prison is a place of punishment, a deprivation of pleasure, a separation from loved ones, a loss of control over events large and small. It suggests the metaphors of darkness: the underworld, the dark of night, the dark night of the soul, an absence that terrifies with its emptiness. It holds the danger of despair. The work of prison *years* is reflection—relentless introspection under a merciless, accusing glare. In this respect prison is a solitary and spiritual place.

But the work of prison *days* is sheer survival—keeping body and spirit intact under the relentless grinding down. What metaphors do we have for using a toilet in a shared room, for stripping in front of a stranger to prove that you harbor no weapons or drugs, for not being hugged good night by your family? The opposite of despair is not hope; it is getting up out of bed every day.

I spent six years in the prison world. I grieved, I despaired, I survived, I rejoiced, I was released.

CONTENTS

SESTINA FOR JAIME

The woman and the boy look back at the years
They have spent together. At what she will leave: the river,
The Santiam that flows cold
From the mountains over its bed of rock
Into the wide Willamette, warm in the summer;
And the sound roof and sturdy walls of their house.

Now that they have more or less deserted this house—
He only sleeps in it; she plans to return in some years—
Now that she will not plan their summer
Around work whose reward is to lifeguard at the river,
Now that she is walled behind an official sort of rock,
And he has come to find the water uninvitingly cold,

He remembers her holding back, afraid of the cold
Water, reading instead on the boat dock; how the house,
A few hours each day, got painted; and the rock
Cliff with its rope where for years
His friends had swung out over the river
Into the deep pools of summer.

She remembers him in the freedom of summer,
And his friends, teeth chattering from the cold
Plunge into the green flow of the June river,
When he alone could coax her from the house
Where she hid out, from what, for years,
He did not know. Their life was like the rock

Walls of the Santiam Canyon, he thought: Rock,
River, Mother, Son, sun, swimming, living for the summer.
She thought they had all the years
Of their lives to buy pizza and cold
Drinks for his friends, pay for painting the house
When they swam too well to need her at the river.

1

She dreams she has become the flow of the river,
And, basking in sun, that she has always been rock,
That she once tried to keep house,
Baking cookies for a human boy. He dreams it is summer,
That he still has a mother holding back from the cold,
And watching, watching him. It has been years

Since he painted the house in summer.
He loads another log into the stove against the cold.
He's added a Zen garden of plants and river rock. It took him years.

2

CLOUDY, WIND GUSTS
TO 25 MPH

GEESE

I sat in the back of the US Marshal's sedan, on the way to Federal Court, my ankles shackled and hands cuffed behind my back since the warrant that accompanied us described me as an escape risk. I wore a black wool suit and pumps but was barelegged because my pantyhose had failed to make it through the prison's cumbersome property procedures in time. The November morning was sunny and bright, and all I cared about at that moment was catching a glimpse of the pond.

My husband had told me about the half-acre pond during a visit. The water displaced from wetlands in the construction of the prison's newest building had formed it just outside the main gate, and now it was home to a year-round population of Canada geese. It made me think of the flights of geese that used to come in low over our back yard in Oregon, still looking for the wetland that had been drained for the building of our house 40 years earlier.

I wanted to see the geese and the way they gather by the dozens in places where they know they are safe from hunters. I wanted to hold in my heart a picture of the cattails and tall grasses. I wanted to be able, just a little, to see this place as the geese see it. To the geese, this pond has become home. For countless generations of them, the wetlands were a place to rest and feed on their migration south for the winter and back north for nesting in spring. But now, after two decades of mild winters, the geese live here year round. I wonder sometimes, how exactly did they make that change?

Geese are among the most intelligent of birds, and like most intelligent species, they are quick to take advantage of new conditions. But, like humans, geese form long-mated pairs and stable social groups capable of passing a culture of acquired information. The old uncle at the head of the V of migrating honkers carries knowledge from generations of forebears, knowledge of waterways and weather patterns, nesting grounds and food supplies.

So, who decided to make this Massachusetts pond the end of the trip? Was it the old uncle, the weight of his moral authority overcoming the anxieties that urged the flock farther south as the days shortened? Or was it some young and confident upstarts who dared to defy the elders and do something new? Were there divorces, mother geese staying behind with their rebellious offspring, fathers tearing themselves away in fear for the very survival? Did the traditionals stop in on their way back north to check on the stay-behind cousins? One thing is sure. Whether migrating or overwintering, the geese on the pond that November day knew a lot more about where they were than I did. To me, this spot between the place I have been and the place I will return to, could be anywhere on the planet.

Imprisoned here, I haven't traveled the roads past local stores and factories where my neighbors work, or the surrounding towns where my co-workers make their homes. I don't know the swimming holes or the best riffles in the rivers on which to cast a wet-fly before a waiting trout. I don't know the shapes and stories of the valleys, bluffs, and buttes that may surround me. I know that the city of Worcester is nearby, so I study the weather maps on the TV news for clues.

I'm the one who decided to break up my family's rhythms, east for hunting in October, to the mountains for skiing in December, out on the river for fishing in April, digging in the garden dirt in July. I am the one who decided that this prison next to a Massachusetts pond would have to be my place for a while. Is the moral authority of my reasons enough to overcome the anxieties of my husband and son? Will there be a divorce, as they create a new pattern of their days without me? Will they continue to stop in on their way through their year to check on me?

I have lived here through a round of seasons now. I have watched snow pile up, then melt. Each day, I listen for the honk of the geese and for the swoosh of letters sliding beneath my door at mail call.

SUNDAY

my cellmate asleep, Sunday breakfast in the day room: cinnamon toaster pastries, an orange, a cup of instant coffee, then another. Undemanding company. "Good morning." "Watch my bag of food for me." Expecting no real answer as I read my magazine.

Ironing, gathering everything of mine and everything of hers that I can find to iron, remembering Sunday breakfast from all the pieces of my life. Always a special Sunday breakfast: bacon, eggs, and sweet rolls from my childhood home; crumb buns and Cafe Bustelo on a stripped and Varathaned maple table from the Salvation Army, Jarlsberg and mushroom omelets with English muffins and bloody marys (alcoholic reality nicely masked by the quest for the perfect recipe); croissants with strawberry cream cheese from the famous patisserie on the corner, laid lovingly on antique plates; corn flour pecan waffles with peach preserves, a test recipe for the cookbook.

6

[INSATIABLE, MY EYES]

Insatiable, my eyes
rake November's ground
as I walk the square—

on the sidewalk, tannic
ghosts laid down by rain
on last night's leaves.

Fine, bright new-growth grass
bends in the wind as if
bowing to

the brown and curling leaves
trapped against the fence
by those same gusts.

Beyond the east fence the red-
berried ornamental I know
not by its name, but by its toxic

roots, the one—do you recall?
that retarded our red onions
in Halsey. Just so

your sleeping back once fed my gaze,
pale northern flesh relaxed across
hard work-built muscle

on that November afternoon
when we should have been grouse
hunting at the river.

SNOW SKY

Dusted limb, branch, twig, near black,
fractalled against a monochrome of whited grey

the masked sun sets, imperceptible
till photo-cell timed lights
flare in a prison yard

deeper and deeper grey the wintry dusk sets in
at five
at half past four...
Attention called to some indoor task
I turn my back,
turn back and it is done
and Solstice night begun.

DAY 400 OF THE RULE "NO SITTING ON THE GRASS"

In the camps they will tell you
no one stays hungry
forever. Sooner or later you stop
desiring, then feeling, believing. Starvation
sets in, and if cool green grass by magic
appeared, So what? your tired shoulders
would shrug. You would mill around the packed dirt
hollow-eyed—

Someday will you lead me to the river's edge,
stub my toes until they bleed
on the tumbled rocks,
hold me knee-deep in snow melt
till my skin burns red
and the high sun raises blisters
on my back. Lay me on the gravel bank
to dry. And if I come alive,
take me home.

WEDNESDAY

*"You are undergoing a great purification,"
P— wrote. "Expect to be uncomfortable sometimes."
I understood; his words call back the remembered
understanding. Before embarking on this
purification, I, as a hero, prepared myself. "I'm
going into the desert," I said. "I'm going alone and
naked through an ordeal, facing dragons (but I will
have my magic sword or some other weapon),
wandering as if lost (but I will have my true vision for
compass, the internal coherence of spiritual journey
for a map). Conditions may be harsh but I'm
accustomed to deprive myself of soft comforts." I
thought, though, that I would have my body, the
earth, my soul. How could I have known, prepared
for the great dullness of this no beauty, no affection,
no aliveness? The very ordinariness trips me. I was
ready for torture and the Quest for Meaning. Instead,
everyday life confined in shoes and a bra, closed by
my macho hero-ness to would-be friends,
resurrecting the skills of leaving behind the loved
ones.*

SNOW, LOW NEAR ZERO

JULY 3

*I am huddled on the floor at the wire grating
of my door, to record this conversation between Joan
Santos and Officer Canali, at her door. We are all
locked down because Joan has threatened, in her
paranoia, to cut herself with a razor:*
    CANALI—How are you doing?
    JOAN—Are you going to let her hurt me?
    *CANALI—No one is going to hurt you. I'm
just going to talk to you, keep you company.*
    *(I see Canali's left leg kick out with a jerk.
His Tourette's syndrome forces a sort of half-bark
past his vocal chords.)*
    JOAN—What's the matter with your face?
    *CANALI—I have a disability. People can
have a disability and still work.*
    *A few minutes later, Joan is holding a razor
at her wrist. Five COs, a nurse, a sergeant, and a
credibly sympathetic lieutenant are outside her door,
ready for any contingency with cuffs, leg irons, and
the Plexiglas shield that will protect them in the event
of a forced move. They talk her into putting the razor
down and take her out of the cell to be housed in the
Hospital Services Unit for a few days.*

July 6

    *Lots of action on the corridor today. Joan
went out to court, trying to get visitation rights with*

11

*her kids when she gets out next month. Officer W—
found a razor hidden in her mattress. They didn't
even bring her back up here when she got back from
court. She went straight to Maximum Security where
a few of the two dozen other incorrigible women will
scream obscenities all day and all night and smear
their walls with excrement. I heard that she won at
court.*

July 7

*After an hours-long lockdown we see the
ambulance pull up to the front gate and leave with
siren singing. We learn that Joan is dead, a suicide,
and no one will ever have to worry about her
paranoia again.*

*The difference between Joan's adventure of
this life and mine seems a matter of a hair's breadth
only, of a different outcome at one key point, one that
left me surrounded by loving help and her alone in
Max.*

THREE POEMS ON A PRISON SUICIDE

I.

You were not sentenced to die
hanged
by a thin shred of jailhouse bathrobe
from a louvered vent
high up enough that you had to climb.

You have to be really serious
about dying
to pull that off.

How exactly did you plan it
so that
the body's emphatic resistance
to dying
was quiet enough?

Or was there just
so much noise
that no one heard
your dying gasps' increment?

I thought I saw you
in the face of a petunia
in the flower bed outside my door
through my tears
this afternoon.

II.

napalm fléchette phosphorous 2-4d free-
fire zone carpet bombing
There sounds a roar as of a hot wind

a cry of grief big as the universe
as of a mother for her newly dead
child, instead, the mother dead. Ed
says Isn't it time to come home
from the war?
as though it were a thing in the past
only, not last
Friday night's singular
melodic strain against the chord.

Some news is not reducible
to bit streams on a fiber optic cable.
It needs a vessel
capable of pain,
needs an archangel's vision
and one small woman's
fist-sized heart.

III.

Taken as a mass, they have no proper name,
LBJs—little brown jobs the birders say.
Ah, but hold just one
for a long moment in your sight
and note, as might a seeking mate,
near perfect symmetry of brown hooded head
barred black-brown-lightest grey wing
tweeded breast.

Desire will draw you back,
your will or no.

CHINA

It must be 90° in here, with the heat from the floor and the heat from the ceiling and the sun pouring in. Sweat runs between my shoulder blades under a black sweatshirt; the sweat under the nosepieces of my glasses loosens them till they slide right off my face. The nurse practitioner says I should take hormones for hot flashes, but how am I supposed to tell what's a hot flash and what's just another March afternoon in a west-facing room with locked windows? I try to focus on the page in front of me, the one I am going to fill with the 500 daily words I am committed to writing. It's all coming out empty and stupid, false start after false start.

Accountable economics, complex adaptive systems and social change, a sestina of failed marriage, even a sketch of the grids of the heavy-weight window screen—anything but what I won't write, which is how it felt to come back from a clinic appointment at 10:30 this morning to find the Special Security in my room, rifling through my correspondence in their latex gloves, making notes.

"Go wait in the dayroom, Miss Power," they told me. So I went and found a *National Geographic* and studied a drawing of temperature patterns of the oceans, the whole story of weather and climate in 2 X 3 inches of glossy paper. I get a lot of letters from a lot of people. They were still going through them long after all the other inmates had been locked down for the 11:30 count. There is a kind of privilege when you get to stay out then, like being one of the big kids in a family after all the little kids have been sent to bed. Eventually they came and told me to go back to my room. They never told me what it was all about, and I am trying to imagine that it didn't really happen because that is easier than tasting the powerlessness you have to swallow.

Now the writing is interrupted by a big drama on the phone—China has escaped from the locked unit of the psychiatric hospital where she was sent after her third suicide attempt here. She charmed one of the male attendants into leaving a door unlocked yesterday and is supposed to be on her way to some place in Florida that he set her up with. Of course he rolled over the minute they held the prospect of jail over his head. That explains this morning's room raid—I am the Vietnam war radical, and she was the Cambodian refugee. There is a certain logic in thinking that I might want to abet her.

We all troop to the other dayroom to watch it on the TV news. They call her a cold-blooded murderer; they say she shot her gang-leader, dope-dealer boyfriend. She told us that he beat her and said he would kill her if she left him. The DAs looked at her closets full of fancy clothes, her size-three body, her face like a doll, her thick black hair down to her ass. They don't believe her; they want to know why she didn't go the police. When she was six, she watched the soldiers in their uniforms shoot her uncle; then they took her father away, and he never came back. I'd say that pretty much explains it.

She and her mother and her little brother walked across Cambodia and down Vietnam. Every place they camped, her mother scrounged up vegetables and sometimes a little meat. She cooked up a pot of soup, put it on her head, and carried it to the nearest crossroads to sell by the bowl to the

16

other ones who were running away after losing their uncles and their fathers, and to such merchants, keepers, and helpers as were hungry for supper and felt like spending a few pennies. They got on a boat across the sea to America and ended up in a three-decker in Dorchester, where, her mother thought, they would finally be safe. I used to see them in the visiting room, the mother my age, the brother all grown up now, and China's own little boy not yet old enough to be in school. Her mother once told her that if she had known how it would all turn out, she would not have tried so hard.

There was another refugee here few years ago, a Hmong woman. We used to walk the square for fitness (6½ times around equals a mile), she in her fine black leather boots and me in my Adidas, talking about nutrition. She had been raped by a gang member and gone back the next day and killed him. One October day she said to me, "Most Asians have died inside, you know." "From the war?" I asked. "Yes," as if it were as ordinary as oak leaves on the ground. I found myself on my knees at the foot of a yard tree, my face scraped by its bark, sobbing. "I tried," I said.

I want to remember that she said, "I know," and that it was like cool balm on my burnt heart. But in fact, I had to collect myself before the yard guard noticed. We went on walking the square until it was time to be sent indoors for lockdown and count.

We live here with dramas extreme, but they are ordinary to us—suicide attempts, rapes, beatings, escapes, blah, blah, blah. Some stories I look at and don't see how they can possibly come out with happy endings. That is the real reason the authorities have no reason to worry that I would help China escape.

GangRape

Your rage, indeed. You raped out your rage
on my Aunt Marie
and left her in a catatonic dread
until she died
three months later.

You say in passing that you sometimes thought
about her feelings
while your brothers spent their rage
on my Aunt Marie
and the others.

I want to make my hand into a fist
and fuck it past your tongue
down through your lungs, your belly, and your bowels
into some place
where you still feel.
I want to trespass against you
as you trespassed against her.

I will believe in absolution when
I see your eyes
as pale pools of horror at her hell;
when for atonement
you bear witness:

sack-clothed and ashen, clutch at all who pass
to tell the story
of you and her and history and rage.

FRIDAY

*S—just read to me from the Angolite, a story
of an executed man whose body was frozen and sliced
into slabs to be electronically scanned and stored as
data. They called him "The Visible Man." I cannot
bear the weight of this knowledge. Days like this I
feel raw, as if naked and sunburned I were
wandering on the lava beds. If I keep moving, the
beating-down sun and the necessary agility feel good.
But the moment I am still....*

*I know too much. The suffering is everywhere
I look. The suffering is mine; the suffering is the
Universe: Alcatraz Aborigines Marbled Murrelet
locked up crazy women fights among the feminists
endwords for a sestina for Persephone—under,
wander, lavender, fear, fall, river*

TEETH

*"We don't do root canals here. I can give you penicillin
and make an appointment to pull the tooth next week."*
                                    -Dr. B—, DDS

It seems we don't suffer enough.
Do you think teeth will show them?
Here! Volunteers—we need teeth—
who's going first?

From a smile spread like ivory
against black walnut,
an incisor.

One, glad to be rid of an ache, threw
the culprit in, she thought—
till the throbbing started up
again. She yanked another
and relief relaxed her
for an hour or so. But when
it boomed again, she drew the line:
"Mine," she said. "Small. And yellow. But mine."

"God, spare our front ones," prayed
the ones who would work.
Who'd want a gap-toothed waitress?

From the tooth that anchored her fine, white bridge
one cracked off a piece, her share,

and tossed it on the pile, one more loss
in a sea of loss, and went back
to bed.

The one who'd come in as a young bride
wept for the hag grin that would greet
her husband when, the ordeal done,
they met again.

Jealous of her wholeness, the last
hung back. But the plate had passed
from hand to hand exempting only
the toothless and those younger than twenty
who had lost one or more
already, on the street.
And it was not yet full. Bitter, she spat out
a molar, probed the socket where the
the spirochetes would thrive,
and dreamed of implants.

We passed them out the slot in the door
like little coins, currency of our losses.
But out there they were busy with their fears.
They dropped the dish, the evidence
scattered, crunched beneath their boots.
"More suffering," they muttered.

We started on the children.

DOPE FIEND

Pray to every power you know that you never have to ask a dope fiend that you love, "What the hell kind of relapse behavior is this?" It doesn't matter how you love a dope fiend, like a lover, like a friend, like a mother, like a son, sooner or later it will seep into your consciousness before you even shape the words. You'll hear the gossip. "Oh, I saw your friend down at the bar the other night." And you stop trusting this gossip who brought you the news. "She's just trying to get between us," you say. "What was she doing down there her own self?" And you wonder if the gossip is going to pick up because that's easier than paying attention to what's been right there to see. The little change in driving habits. She stops short, crawls up someone's bumper, leans on the horn, cuts the left turns a little close for comfort. Or a change in routine. She stops working out. Or she works out twice a day seven days a week. She takes up smoking again. She lies. Just about something little, something too trivial to matter. "I forgot," she says, when something doesn't get done. And maybe she's forgotten a hundred times before, but this one is different. She borrows money. "I didn't get to the ATM." It's not even for dope yet. It's just the hustle setting itself up. And the worst thing is, you know all this because she has told you herself late at night with the lights out, along with every other secret of her soul. Your life together changes. Instead of dinner at home with friends, it's more nights out, more new people, someday there's a stranger in your kitchen making coffee. There's an acronym for denial they teach in every drug program.

Don't

Even

kNow

I

Am

Lying.

And by now you're lying, and she's lying, and no one is looking at the elephant in the room. Because what then?

I remember when the first dope fiend I really cared about got sent back to prison. Candy was her name. Big and sloppy fat, cast in one eye, wild hair. Her grandmother loved her, and sometimes when she talked, you could believe that might be enough. I used to sit with her, working on the reading comprehension questions she was developing, and I would wonder, Where will she fit in? I would cry just a little film of tears (Prozac, you know) because I couldn't see a place for her in that world out there, no matter how optimistic and creative I could get. When she came back, I didn't want to look at her. I acted like we never had met. Just like that, closed up my heart and wrote her off. Never did speak to her. She went out to the street two more times, and came back one. She didn't come back the second time because her heart exploded on a bench in a park where the crackheads hang, and she died. You would think that would cure me of loving dope fiends.

I got wary. I limited my investment. Time, maybe, but no heart. Teach reading, but don't love. Help plan a future, but don't believe. Dope fiends came and went. I heard, "Such-and-so OD'd the day

24

after she hit the street." And I didn't even remember what Such-and-so looked like, even though she'd been here three times in four years and I had played soccer with her in the prison gym.

But the brown eyes that looked straight into mine, the clowning with a cut-off sweatpants leg worn as a hat (boy, was that against the rules), the 50 pushups off the bed, the 20 pushups she got out of me—who wouldn't get reckless again?

There's a certain kind of person that loves a dope fiend. It's not just their woundedness; it's the bravery and the crazed hope in the face of it all. I have radar for it. I always catch them when they're sober, since I'm no masochist, and I am sure not a rescuer. I didn't even recognize the pattern until after the fourth one, sixth if you count alcoholics.

I can already feel the judgment closing in on my heart. I can feel my back getting ready to turn. I want to be wrong, so I let my mouth and my pen talk eloquently. But in my heart, I am already gone, surviving, buying a blow dryer and some Paul Mitchell mousse. Because I can be beautiful all by myself, if I have to. Because life is easier this way. Because if it wasn't this time, it would be another.

[I AM ALIVE]

I am alive—
too alive
in this mid-February thaw
of coarse-grained icy snow grotesques
running a river bed
of sidewalk edge and earthen bank
toward a silted delta at the drain

too alive for this place of don't touch
don't love,
of husband, lover three thousand miles
away
from my tensed thighs
full lips
aching belly
breasts loose beneath a sweatshirt colored dark
to catch the cross-quarter sun's heat

too alive
for this cell filled with memory
(too near obsession)
of taboo flesh glimpsed
between shirt and jeans,
of waved black hair and dark brown eyes.

26

SHOWERS, HIGH NEAR 55

SATURDAY

Another hungry day. I almost got myself in trouble over green beans. It was supposed to be cabbage—that's the only reason I went up to the serving room. But we were last, and they had run out. They weren't going to give us any vegetable at all, just the gray-brown oval of mystery meat and some white rice, red jello for dessert, melted in the heat, and we're supposed to eat it with a fork. "You can't just skip the vegetables," I was hollering at the Food Service guy. "You can't." I stood there with my fork and my napkin and didn't move, didn't take a tray, just kept looking at him. The Fork Officer asked what was the holdup, and I told him I was waiting for the vegetables. He told the Food Service guy to do something about it, told me to take a tray and they would bring me vegetables. I sat down at the table, gave the meat away like always, and started to eat the rice. In a minute the Food Service guy brought out a soup bowl of canned green beans he had heated in the staff dining room microwave.

Monday
Sally came last night, a surprise visit. I asked one favor, near the end of the visit.
"Please write down for me the daily ration for someone in a refugee camp. I know there is a range—just something typical." Sally has worked in

international famine relief for years. "Why?" she asked.

"When I am angry because I am hungry, when I am hungry because I can't eat the food, I want to remember that I am only feeling the privation of a fat, well-fed American. It will help me with the anger."

"I think you are asking the wrong question. You don't have to excuse your suffering because someone else's is worse. You don't have to.... You must have so much.... I'm just being psychological here. I always used to...."

The stream of words stops. She looks directly in my eyes and pulls these words from that never-before-spoken place: "Their daily ration is the love and the touch of their community. I have watched them. They die; they grieve; they sing; they bury their dead. And they touch one another. They are always touching one another."

I bend my head to my arms on the visiting room table. She touches the top of my head with her whole palm (forbidden). "So cry," she says, "but not for the vegetables. Cry for your losses. Cry."

EXILE, APRIL

At home the daffodils have naturalized
and grow like weeds
bright yellow
in the grass seed fields

rhododendrons I do nothing at all for
give pale purple double blooms
in profusion for a month

the yellow climbing rose
once hacked to the ground by a helpful neighbor
yields buds for the altar
from April to December

SATURDAY

My lower back hurts all the time, especially when I sit at the desk. Walking today, I walked faster and faster, trying to outwalk it. Logic and my little knowledge of backs and why they hurt say, "Silly idea." But my intuition nagged me to believe it. If nothing hurt, would I make up something? Or maybe the pain—in my back, or in my heart—shows up and the brain concocts a reasonable story to explain it. When M— was leading the meditation and yoga group, she suggested the possibility of "no story," not just a truer one in place of a false or incomplete one. That's detachment. I could stand to be more detached from my pains. The danger is becoming detached from my pleasures and joys. Deadly ground for me. I must somehow break the habit of sleeping to escape the overwhelming afternoon pain. Perhaps a system of reward—cookie, candy, mocha—at 4:00 if I get through without sleeping? That is a real possibility. I can feel it. I can envision it: pain and sorrow overwhelming me, pushing me toward escape via sleep. Held at bay, pushed back by the promise of Vienna Fingers! What number of Vienna fingers is the breakeven? Not one, for sure. Four. For four Vienna Fingers I could say no to that sorrow. Instead, I would sit, breathe, notice. To be practical, I'll have to have someone hold the cookies for me. If I held them, I would just find an excuse to eat them all up. Thirty-two cookies per package, $2.69. Eight days a week, as the Beatles might say.

RIVER

I heard this story today: Two guys who work at the youth psychiatric facility are playing basketball near the river. A girl-woman with many troubles, known to them, walks by. They hear a scream, see that she is nowhere, run over to the riverbank. There she is, ten feet down, holding on to a clump of roots, dangling above the winter riverflow. One goes for help; one stays. The one who stays talks to her—quiet, hold on, talk to me. He can't reach her. He can't rescue her. Being Christian, he says, "Do you want me to pray with you?" He means this with the most tender, generous heart. She will probably die, he thinks. How can he watch a many-troubled girl-woman slip away to drown, tumbled in currents that float whole uprooted trees down to the sea? And she knows she is dying. That there never has been anyone to rescue her from dangers—from stepfathers and strangers with knives, from the cold or the dark. Why would anyone show up to save her from a moment's misjudged footing on a muddy riverbank? It's been a long time coming, this slip.

She grows quiet. Her shivering stills. Her fingers let go. She drops past the undercut bank into the brown river that, even dammed upstream for dry season water supply, has plenty to wrap her in.

Seven minutes later the ambulance arrives. The young man's sister is afraid he is growing hard of heart.

Sometimes I think it's the girl-woman who's dropped off the side of the river bank, and me trying to hold on to her with nothing but words of comfort.

But sometimes I know it's me holding on to nothing but roots, and my hands are numb and stinging at the same time, and that moving, mindless water, might be where I will finally belong.

WASHING THE BITTERNESS OUT

Life could hang on a shred of garbage. I sat slumped in a flimsy plastic chair in the dayroom. Inner fog weighed my face into heavy-muscled immobility, this dullness a final retreat from the sadness about nothing, about everything, that is depression. I had walked up to the serving room for dinner but eaten nothing. The bread was like cotton and the peas like paste in my mouth. I lacked the energy to walk the rest of the way to my cell. Once I would have wondered how I would live through the night. By now I knew I didn't have the drive it takes to defeat my billion body cells in their millions-of-years-evolved, organ by organ determination to go on living.

C— sat across from me, a spiral of orange and white uncurling onto the table from her fingers. Droplets of oil escaped from the peel's bruised cells to fill the air around us with the perfume of another world entirely. She gathered up the peel and was about to throw it into the trash. "Don't waste that," I said. "Let me have it. I'll make candy." The words hurled themselves as if memory had tossed a lifeline across the gap between me and all that was living. I got up from the chair.

Within minutes I had half a dozen oranges. They were available everywhere in trade for cigarettes, which had become scarce since the prison canteen stopped selling them two weeks before. My cellmate had stockpiled, and at that time she was probably the richest person in the prison economy. I asked permission to use the inmate kitchen at the end of the corridor and spread my *mise-en-place*

33

across the counter: sugar, oranges, colander, brown paper grocery bag torn open, laid flat, and sprinkled with sugar to receive the finished product. I managed to keep everyone else out of the kitchen through a combination of acutely territorial body language and the promise of tastes when I finished. I began the rhythmic ritual, the almost-prayer that is the attention to raw food, the knowledge in my hands, the practice controlling pan and heat, the instructions of the recipe, read twenty years ago and often written down for friends.

"Cut off the polar caps and score the orange peel right through to the flesh in perfect meridians a quarter of an inch wide at the equator. Peel back the strips of skin gently enough that they don't crack."

This being a medium security prison, where sharp objects are carefully controlled lest they be used for stabbing, I cut with a plastic knife and was grateful for it. The fruit went into a re-used plastic Cool Whip bowl to become salad, along with apples my cellmate will buy for cigarettes and the banana promised on tomorrow's breakfast menu.

"In a saucepan with a large surface, cover the strips of peel with cold water. Bring to a boil on high heat, and simmer for eight minutes. Drain, re-cover with cold water, and repeat twice more."

This step washes the bitterness out and is as old a cooked food itself. The acorns that sustained humans for thousands of years are so full of bitter tannins that they are poisonous unless boiled in just this way.

"After the three leachings, return the strips to the saucepan and cover them with an approximately equal amount of sugar, adding just enough water to

34

dissolve it. Cook them in this syrup over medium-high heat until they absorb it, about twenty-five minutes. Stir frequently to keep the syrup from scorching in the hot spots on the bottom of the pan."

During this final cooking I like to arrange the strips in a circular array around the pan, curves all aligned, orange toward the outside, white toward the center to keep the peels from being bent backwards and breaking. But if it started out merely practical, this step holds me by its beauty. It's like calculating the harmonics required to keep a bridge from swaying to the breaking point, only to come up with a Beethoven trio sonata.

"Drain the peels of the last bit of syrup and spread them on the sugar-covered brown paper. Sprinkle with additional sugar to keep them from sticking together in a clump. If you have your own kitchen, drain them and let them air dry on waxed paper; they will form finer crystals and be more delicate."

I cleaned up my mess in the kitchen, put some of the candy aside for my cellmate and myself, and gave the rest away to the other thirty women in my housing unit. In less than an hour I had come back from the brink of living death. The orange's nutritious flesh is no match for anhedonia. But the peel, with its pigments and its oils, the essence of what we think of as "orange," too bitter by itself, is reclaimed by a technique older than history, bathed in sugar, arranging itself into a miniature of the sun in my pan.

PRECIOUS PLEASURES

One dozen cuts of just-tender bright green bean
(The taste of summer startles me
from twelve minutes at a prison lunch table
to Willamette Valley evenings
staking and picking Blue Lakes with you)

ten thick-cut carrot rounds, served hot

three mallard ducks against the eleven a.m. sky
on Thursday

three friends sharing coffee after Jello-doused white
frosted cake
from the lady magazine

* * *

Last night Hazel cooked for me in Brattleboro,
"Life Soup" she called it.
She blessed sautéing onions,
chopped in a good bunch of kale
and two yellow Finn potatoes,
and thought of me
in my prison. She knows
I live now on the offerings of believers
and the occasional perfect green bean.

36

FRIDAY

Some days all I need is to see a hillside of chicory flowers. Like a dog, like a bird—like the living things, I am on the earth. Sun loves me; breeze embraces me. My breasts feel heavy....

PREACHER

She's a showman, so I'm sure she wouldn't mind if I used her real name, and her self as the actor. But I can't. I can't just put her out there. She's not mine to use like that. I have to come up with a name with the same rhythm, different vowel pattern, maybe ending in "i". The name is not a trivial issue.

You can't just call someone like this Maria. For one thing, Maria is a traditional, not a made up, name. Our friend definitely has a made up name. Imagine how different her life might have been if she'd had the kind of mother (and even, if you can imagine, father!) who would name a child Maria. Besides being traditional, it is distinctly feminine. And there is nothing distinctly feminine about her, unless maybe you could see her with her clothes off, which I never have. She is ambiguous as to gender, she is ambiguous as to race, and she never stops dancing.

I can still see her playing the part of a pastor in the Black History Month show: satin choir robe, boots poking out at the bottom. For a second I pictured a microphone in her hand, but there was no microphone, and she never needed one. She has a preacher's voice, a preacher's unchoked voice calling out the story of salvation and damnation. "I believe," one hand raised to the sky, fingers spread wide. "Do you believe?" And the congregation shouts, "We believe."

She stomps off the paces from the left to the right side of the imaginary sanctuary on the stage of the prison gym. She stops, points accusation at one congregant, and starts. "I know. Yes, I know that you've been judgin' your sisters," her elbows bent, arms flapping against her sides. "I know," the accusing finger again, "that you have had gossip in your heart and the name of one of our sisters in your mouth. I know," and she resumes her flapping, boot-stomp pacing, "that you think you are holier than ALL of us." At this she throws her arms wide and brings them around as if she could, really could, embrace that congregation in one hug all at once. "You LEAD the hymn. You READ the Word. You FEED the pastor lunch, and you CLEAN the pastor's house." She is pacing and flapping again, pivot and return on every rhyme. "Yes, you are a GOOD woman. You may even be a GODLY woman. THAT is between you and God. And what is between your sister and God is between your SISTER and God."

Every syllable formed with exaggerated care, the voice reaching out to the back row as strong as when she started. Sometimes I am confused and instead of God being eternal, it's been her, stomping, pacing, flapping, scolding, pointing, reaching for all of time. We are in her power, and it better be a good power because she can play with us any way she will. But part of why we go with her, why we let her take us away is that face—turned up nose, brown eyes round and open as a baby's. You can't tell if she's black or white, man or woman, and that's because she is everything, all the good of all God's everything in one dancing singing package and if she is holy then everything that is like her must be holy too.

There is a world where she's just another dope fiend who held up the Seven-Eleven, crazy hungry on a mission to feed that habit, and anyone in the way is just that—in the way, and better get back. But here she is, blessed with the gift. And if it's not a church but just a stage in a prison gym where she's preaching, we are not confused. If her gift gets no appreciation on Sundays, it's a gift from God anyway. God must surely love her to give her such a powerful gift. And if God loves her like that then maybe God can love us all.

8:30. Lights up. Officer Rose Kelly sounding mad before we ever gave her anything to be mad about. "Ladies, return to your units. Let's go ladies. Final downward movement."

GODWIND

"The goal of spiritual direction is to develop in the directee
a personal relationship with god."
-Sister Ann

A gust so strong
I smelled the lilacs from beyond
the fence—
You lifted me up from my place
at the top of the prison yard steps,
revealed Yourself to me
and for an instant
We wore down the face of rock and
stirred up ocean waves. Together
made weather,
ripening '87 reds to the rarest of vintages,
freezing continents indiscriminately.
Returned,
my feet take the pavement steps to the yard.

SPLIT COMPLEMENTS

Loop upon loop of razor wire
like the ovals we practiced for perfect penmanship
remind me that in the nuns' world
everything was ordered. Even the colors
arranged themselves
into a circle of twelve equal parts.

"Orange," Sister Regina said,
"is the complement of blue, and so
the neighbors to either side of it
go particularly well with blue."

Three stories high the maple,
red-orange and yellow-orange
against the Indian summer sky—

The sagging vinyl liner, sky
blue, of the prison's disused
pool, deck carpeted in those same flames.

SUNNY, BREEZY, 80-85

DANGEROUS

I defy the rules
of "Bind your feet" and "Bind your breasts,"
button the State-issue chambray shirt
over bare skin,
walk out into the late-June sun,
sit on the young grass, and dare
to take off my shoes.

On the soles of my feet, grass, rough;
on my nipples, summer heat.
I tense my legs and hold my breath,
tip my hips minutely
and control by a strong act of the will
my arms lifting to embrace,
my tongue and teeth and lips shaped to kiss hard
the casually inviting one
also lying on the grass,
head inches from mine,
body at an angle of 110°
like hands at four o'clock
on a whimsical garden chronometer.

WEEDS

"What are you looking for, Miss Power?" the yard guard asked. It is his job to watch for any sign that an inmate might be ready to break a rule, to fight, to smoke, to receive food from a friend, a lover, or a victim. To escape. He had spotted me walking along with my eyes intently fixed on the "Out of Bounds" side of the grass. He had noticed when I retraced my steps as a pattern my eye had too hastily passed over made its impression on my brain and called attention back to itself.

"I'm looking at the weeds. I'm not going to eat them. I'm just noticing what's growing, what stage it's at." I really have no cool. But then, neither does he have a clue.

"So your interest is purely botanical."

"That's right." Of course my real interest was culinary. I had been hatching a plot. I would volunteer to weed that area, then I would smuggle the edibles back to my housing unit kitchen to cook up with frozen collard greens and bacon from the inmate store.

Nowhere in the prison rules is it written that we are not allowed to eat the weeds. This is not a lapse on the part of the Director of Security. It's just that the rule makers here get their food at the supermarket. They have no more need to notice the purslane that grows in the warmth of the steam vent than I have a need to notice the reflective letters on the green street sign outside the perimeter fence.

You would think I had been through a famine. I watch for wild foods as if my life depended on them. The mustards flower, yellow dots here and there on a north-facing hillside, and I am chagrined to have missed their leaves. I learn again, as I seem to have to learn every year, how very short this season of early weeds is, how intolerant is the natural world of my failure to get out of my winter torpor and get moving on time. I will have to find pleasure in imagining the salad I could make from the season's first Sweet Williams, Johnny Jump-ups, and sorrel. Every time I walk past the violets in the flower beds on my way to my housing unit, I will imagine them candied, garnishing a white-frosted cake.

It is my fourth spring here. The budding branches in sunny warmth against a clear blue sky still provoke a dizzying and deep sense that something is wrong. I find myself worrying how the trees will get all their work done when they haven't blossomed and it's the dry season already. With an effort I remind myself that this is New England, not Oregon, that the trees here know how to follow the harsh contrasts of cold winter, warm spring, hot summer. They know when it is safe to unfurl their leaf buds.

Inside I am still a creature of the cool rainy winter, mild rainy spring, dry warm summer of the Willamette Valley. There, one April, colleagues and I drove up I-5 from Eugene to Seattle for the annual Restaurant Trade Show. Because it was a long distance for a day trip, we started out before dawn. As the daylight grew we found ourselves traveling through a pale, yellowed-green world of grasses in every field and leaves newly opened, gentled against a gray sky, everything softened by a rain that was barely more substantial than a mist. We were wrapped in a quintessential Valley spring.

Sometimes I hated that protracted spring, the worry that rain would rot the strawberries before they could ripen or split the sweet cherries on the tree. I wanted to send my wool-lined parka to the dry cleaner, not keep wearing it right up into June. When I was a child in Colorado, summer solstice was a barely noticed shift from days getting longer to days getting shorter. In the Willamette Valley, it was truly a holy day of celebrating the arrival of reliably hot and sunny weather.

I never expected to be gone from that spring for so long. My lawyers had negotiated a Plea Agreement that promised a transfer from Massachusetts to a prison in Oregon. I thought I had it all under control—prison time, yes, but close to home, son and husband visiting twice a week, familiar sky. The Deputy Commissioner of Corrections finally told my lawyers to stop trying, that no transfer would happen. I became angry, held back, and refused to put down roots. I wanted to hate this place. Some time in the past year I realized I was only withholding nutrients from myself. I let go of the anger and planned to get a plot in the prison Recreation Department vegetable garden. After all, they are only annuals.

46

THURSDAY

The garden is like something in a refugee camp—the hodge-podge of seeds brought by well-meaning helpers who don't know about the sandy soil; the lack of tools, the difficulty with water, the poor germination, the ants, the aphids. It's not so much about food—calories and nutrients—as about the idea of food, the memory of food, the promise of food. The green and wax beans the other night were beautiful, but maybe I am just defeated, worn out by what it takes to keep memory of the free world where you buy your own seeds or save them from year to year, or get Sicilian garlic cloves from your friend's immigrant in-laws in Cleveland...

Sometimes it all just seems to be too lean to give an abundant outcome no matter how I juggle. Maybe I am just being ungrateful. Or maybe I am being grateful, grateful for the pitiful little we have, seeing it clearly, without denial or romanticizing, taking in the green beans, the chance to walk barefoot on dirt, to squat in sunlight and dig with rocks and sticks, to feel defeated one day, surprised and even delighted the next, when three teensy cucumbers show themselves behind the first female flowers.

AUGUST

The red kale grows like rose petals.
A hint of petunias carries on the breeze.
The blue chicory flower I tasted on the sly
surprises me with blandness.
Like some blue-hided ungulates
on the Serengeti Plain
we gather in the sparse shade of trees
under the midday sun,
and as the evening cools, spread out.

I'm not ashamed to pray willy-nilly thanks
for shreds of cloud and for the late-day sun
that glints off the fuselage of a 737.
I worship water equally in lakes
or gushing from the tap against a spoon
in whorls, eddies, and gurgles
like a brook in the Connecticut woods.

WATERMELON

It was a good summer for watermelon, long and hot. The vines in our patch flourished, the little yellow male blossoms dotting them regularly by early August. But our soil was sandy and poor; we had only six female blossoms, identifiable by the bulbous perfectly round baby fruit at their base. Two set small fruits that rotted. Three bore their fruits so late that I had to pick them off and let the plant's energy go into finishing the one fruit that was doing well. And how that one did grow! By mid-September it was twenty inches long and weighed over twenty pounds. I let it grow for as long as I dared, to be sure it was ripe. Finally the rains threatened and I could put off the harvest no longer.

We had two choices about picking the melon. I could sneak a plastic pancake spatula from my housing unit kitchen down to the garden and split the watermelon into five pieces, which we would have to eat on the spot. But the assumption here is that we are all thieves and will steal or strong-arm everything that is not vigilantly overseen. There are rules: No Eating In The Yard. All Garden Produce Must Be Registered With The Rec. Officer Immediately Upon Being Picked. I could not bring myself to commit the flagrant violation of the rules that a watermelon picnic would entail. I decided to go through official channels and ask for instructions on how to proceed.

Picking and dividing a watermelon is not something the prison has an established procedure for. And thinking up solutions to such a problem on the spot is not a strong point among personnel in an organization where order is the highest value. Inevitably, the answer was a little wacky. It only worked at all because the captain who commanded the three-to-eleven shift was a real human being. On the way to dinner I spotted him and proposed my plan: That evening when the yard opened, I would pick the watermelon, cut it up in my unit kitchen and distribute shares to the other gardeners. He countered with instructions to pick it right then and bring it to the main kitchen to be cut up. You don't argue with a shift commander, especially one who is trying to help you achieve a complicated project. I complied.

The Yard Officer hesitated when I asked him if I could go into the off-limits garden area of the closed prison yard right in the middle of dinnertime, citing the captain's orders. But he was no rookie. He made a judgment call about the credibility of my story and escorted me to the garden where I picked the watermelon, hefted it onto my shoulder, and began the walk across the yard. A whole watermelon in an inmate's possession is a shocking sight, enough to make anyone forget her manners. "Hey, where's my piece?" "I know you're going to be passing some of that watermelon my way." Even my escort did not inhibit requests, threats, and harassments as I made my way across the yard. The Yard Officer left me at the institution Building door.

Of course the Corridor Officer stopped me. "Where are you going with that watermelon, Miss Power?" I repeated the captain's instructions; she let me pass. I had to laugh and joke my way past another gauntlet of women who would do a lot to get their hands on a watermelon. Once I got to the serving room, I informed the Officer Who Supervises the Dispensing of Forks of the captain's plan. He put the watermelon on the dumbwaiter and phoned the downstairs kitchen to tell them it was on its way. "Yes, a watermelon. Miss Power grew it in her garden, and now it seems she wants to share it with her friends... She needs it cut into five pieces... Because the captain said so... Yes, just put it in plastic... No, five separate plastic bags, and send it back up."

The job took twenty-five minutes because the inmate kitchen workers had already cleaned up their counters, and all the knives had been checked back in, counted, and locked up for the night. It seemed like hours to me, though, as I waited pressed against the wall, trying to stay out of the way of the last of the women in line for dinner.

"What's on your shirt?" the Fork Officer asked suspiciously when he noticed the mud from the ground-lying side of the watermelon that had caked the right shoulder of my T-shirt. Nothing here goes unremarked. The Door Officer asked the Fork Officer what I was doing there, then hollered the story across the room to the Serving Room Sergeant. "It seems Miss Power grew this watermelon...."

Even when the dumbwaiter bell rang and the five long wedges of color-of-summer watermelon, each in its plastic bag, were handed over, the project was not done. Only one of the garden partners lived in the same housing unit as I did. Now I had to walk all over the yard delivering the other three pieces. We are not allowed to enter any housing unit except our own, so once again I had to face down Officers Guarding Their Doors and repeat the captain's instructions that the watermelon wedges be delivered to the authorized garden-participant inmate. Not one of them actually called the captain to confirm the bizarre story.

At last I was ready to enjoy my own share of the watermelon. I long ago learned that sooner or later you finish the last bite of even the most special treat, and all that's left is the story. I decided that all thirty of the women in my corridor should share the fruit of the summer's sun and the buckets of water we had hauled the fifty yards from the greenhouse to the garden. With a plastic knife I cut it into two-bite chunks, and we partied.

HALF-WILD

Each summer, we were supposed to clean up our garden spot on the last weekend in October, to tidy things up before the seasonal rule Don't Go In the Garden Space was made explicit. But things don't stop growing just because the guards say, "Don't go in the garden space." They have a life of their own. I said I would do it, and I did. But instead of tearing everything out and putting it in garbage bags in the dumpster by the Clinic door, I bent the radishes, lettuces, and tomatoes over and suggested that they reseed themselves. I cracked open the late season watermelons and the cantaloupes we had grown from seed smuggled out of the Central Kitchen garbage and loosed their seeds in the dirt at the edge of the plowed ground, then kissed it all good-bye and waited to see what would happen.

Next May, the Recreation department somehow failed to rent a rototiller, so the square of ground never was turned wholesale. Instead we had to dig the individual plots by hand, sometimes with a shovel, sometimes squatting with nothing but rocks and sticks. By then our plot already had a healthy crop of sorrel, purslane, and four-inch high lettuce. I sprinkled it with dandelion seeds, cleared weeds away from the five volunteer green onions, and dreamed of salad.

All through June we harvested baby lettuces and mild-tasting weeds to dress with mayonnaise from the Canteen store, thinned with garlicky vinegar from the dill pickles sold whole, sharpened with a shake of crushed dried chilies and some Kraft Parmesan. By July 4th radish thinnings added a peppery bite. It's too bad I didn't learn about eating pea shoots until the arrival of the August issue of Food Arts magazine, or we surely would have added them. The poor quality seeds and the sandy, sloping ground kept the pea plants from ever growing more than eight or ten inches tall, and we had simply written them off. This whole thing is one long meditation in allowing yourself to be bent by whatever winds blow. Everything living on this planet got here just this way.

EXIT PLANNING, SEPTEMBER

I'm so ready to be done with the social scene here. It is real work to achieve the meditative state of pure presence. How can you be present when you have no future? In an hour-long walk in the yard tonight, I exchanged not one bit of conversation. It's as if everyone is preparing for the separation by withholding breath from our encounters. I have nothing more to say to anyone; no one has anything more to say to me. The magic moment of being able to see how we are the same has passed. I am faced outward now, toward a life that is foreign not only to the people here, but even to me. What would we talk about? I forget, now, what there ever was to talk about. What happened? I stopped going to Rec when the rules changed to require that we sign up for activities in advance. So close to the end of my time, it was too much bother.

The door will open. It will close behind me.

UNSETTLED,
PARTIAL ECLIPSE 12:15-12:39 A.M.

NOT HOME

I look out the two windows of my room here on T—'s 36 acres of second-growth Douglas fir. The only human-made thing I see is a red stepladder with three safety/danger warnings stuck on it, two with pictures. The moss-covered branches are ghostly in the light fog. At night, moonlight filters down and casts them in silhouette. But I am not moved to that feeling that is like a mother's pleasure at the sight of her child lying across the bed even when, at twelve, he has become hairy-legged and frighteningly masculine. No, I am refusing to love this place.

I loved the last place that I lived. I did hold the winter-bare dogwoods in my gaze, let my arms open and my breast ache to embrace them as a mother might. I walked its paths past the hillsides of a few wild mustards, some chicory, the naturalized violet clusters. I said yes to the strange late-spring unfolding of leaf buds, to a garden of sandy soil, to hoping for an afternoon thundershower, to late-January sun growing strong enough to burn my face, reflecting off the snow. Then I left, and I can never set foot there again.

No wonder I have dreams that a bureaucratic snafu sends me back to prison for a short while. Hades' warning to Persephone was the truth: if you eat anything here, you will never be able to leave the underworld. The pomegranate seed did her in. My downfall was sorrel and purslane, young dandelions and raggedy cucumbers. I cannot go back. Yet I cannot leave that patch that was my people's, where I bargained with the gods of rain and frost, outwitted the demons of hose-control, loved its yield with my whole heart, made sacrament with it, fed it to my surprised and hungry fellow prisoners and finally to a skinny dark-eyed lover.

I called coming back to Oregon coming home. But I will lose the garden patch and the hunting grounds in the divorce, and the riverboat has rotted in the rain. My food comes from the Safeway store. I can have fresh blueberries from Chile in February, corn-fed strip loin steaks. For a while, I have enough money to buy anything. So why am I always hungry? I am getting fat trying to fill this emptiness: croissants, white chocolate, fresh-ground custom blended coffee.

Once, I lived here. I could live here again. I could live anywhere; I've already demonstrated that. It's late February, planting time in the Willamette Valley. I am afraid to poke a single pea seed into the dirt and watch its sprout push skyward, to anticipate the sweetness of the sugar snap pods, to pick and stir-fry and feed them to a friend. I am afraid that before I know it I will be saving a few seeds and bargaining with the demons of pea enation for a fall crop. I never want to lose my people or my land again. I am going slow.

JUNE 22

*I pull out of the Sheriff's substation parking lot
where I stopped in to tell my Probation Officer that I
have moved (as required by the rules that allow me to
live in Oregon). I drive past Roth's. I am not even
tempted to stop. No doughnut, no pillow-soft thing of
icing and silky fat, could touch this pain. It spreads
from my throat closed against tears down across my
chest, my breasts, around my belly. It freezes on my
face.*

*I wanted to say I saw it coming: "If you're
going to work with kids, you have to go through the
state's criminal registry. Since you were convicted in
Massachusetts, you're considered a multistate...[I
forget the exact word—like exact words matter!] You
would have to be fingerprinted and the prints sent to the
FBI. Depending on your crime, you might be prohibited
from working with children forever. For other crimes,
it's twenty years. The process takes about six weeks. We
would be glad to support you through it, but for a
summer job..."*

*I once roughed out an essay titled "Out of
Shame: Receiving Forgiveness." What was I,
delusional? I understand now why R— picked up the
needle. Who would want us, dirty goods that we are?
Will making art out of this keep me alive?*

*I am sitting at a picnic table in the park at the
center of Lebanon, blistered by sun, chilled by breeze.
They don't care who I am. I am entitled, just by being
here. Will sun and breeze and daisy-spotted grass keep
me alive?*

*I have to go get the mail I forgot at my old
house last night, and the files full of bank statements,*

probation fee receipts, and poems. Will mundane chores keep me alive?

   Maybe I'm just too sensitive. Will toughness keep me alive?

NEVER FAR FROM HOME

I don't know how I will live. For what feels like the ten-thousandth time, I am well and truly lost. And of course, when you are lost, it seems as if you will never be found, that like Hansel and Gretel, you cannot imagine finding your way back home. Your fear rises, and your confusion too, to the point where if you did have a map in your pocket, you wouldn't remember. In your panic you might use your remaining reserves of energy running frantically from one meaningless point to another. In your despair you might eat mushrooms or imagine yourself before a house of impossible gingerbread, gumdrop, candy cane sweetness, and begin breaking off pieces and stuffing them into your mouth.

And if you did remember the map and you held it in your hands before your eyes, it would seem to be drawn in old, undecipherable symbols. You would not know that water gushing from a tap against the bowl of a spoon is the same as a small wild water flowing freely over rock. You could not match the sound, heard in the space between waking and sleeping, of the rhythmic rise and fall of air rushing around the intake and exhaust vents, crashing against the semicircle of brick enclosure, to the rhythm of the waves breaking beyond the dunes all night as you once slept under the stars.

Perhaps the map is written in the language of the future. If you only knew enough of its grammar, you could connect the stories of electrical and chemical goings-on in your brain with the time-and-place you came from, back through bargainings over kills on the savannah, through the red of ripened

60

fruit means food, through the shoots of this and the roots of that mean food, back to the Mother of all living things, whom your people named Mary, back even before that to the Ancestor of the Mother of all living things, rock itself, who might be known as Ann, one of the names your people gave you, thinking only that it was euphonious with your daily one. All this you could learn from the map, but could it take you home if you were lost?

More likely, the map is as easy to read as the back of your hand, but you can't make it out for the enchantment that envelops you like fog. Do you know how fog blinds? You would at first think that it is a mere veil, a shimmer of opacity between your eye and the landscape. But no—it is a maze of droplets befuddling your mind's usual rapid computation of reflected-light-into-meaning with strange refractions, so that you can't tell where you are and you miss the boat landing where you meant to take out because it seems as if you must be on another river entirely, not your familiar Willamette. It is worse than the darkness of a new-moon night.

You would have only to cock your ear at the first, faintest honking from a V of geese a full half-minute away from the section of sky in your range of vision; or raise your face and let your arms follow their impulse to open wide at a breakthrough of late January sunlight, surprisingly strong; or believe your astonished nose and eyes when you encountered wild onions among the grass in a Bronx park; or taste in your captivity a single olive, salt-bitter-sour-oily-thick around your tongue, and remember sprouting from ancient rocks in a land you have never been to but know exists. Maybe you would even try to sing your way back home with poems.

I was born knowing. But like most of us who live indoors, I was quickly untaught. My people were herded into the cities and towns, from Languedoc, from Cork, from Prince Edward Island. My grandfather knew the name of every major peak from Cheyenne to Santa Fe; my grandmother gathered chokecherries and, in alternate years, piñons. But my mother calls every tree with needles "just a pine," and thinks that vegetables for dinner come from the frozen food aisle at Safeway.

In my years as a chef and restaurateur, food guided me. Food—raw from the dirt, or in the storage forms of dried beans, fermented juices, ground grains, precious oils, even cheeses and the flesh of the creatures of the land, water, and air—food, along with hungry people, holds the whole story. Still, I live in this time-and-place, and being a social animal, I can be beguiled into the competition for certain status, believing that it would secure food for my self and my child. I can forget that food comes from the land, not the bank account, as easily as the next one. Our birthright is this: to be needed for what we can do, and to be fed.

I am between homes, landless and without community for now. Much more than my time in prison, this is time in the desert. In this time of living in a city full of transplanted trees, it is hard work to keep my spirit up. I hang on to a few poems from the prison years, where we dug the garden dirt with rocks, sticks, and bare hands, and celebrated as sacraments yellow squashes, radish pods, and black-seeded Simpson lettuce reseeding itself.

INCIDENT

The day they hanged Ken Saro-Wiwa
the chores called to me anyway,
knife-sharp hoe and battered radio
to the field beyond the back yard.

Chop. The handle's arc blinks out the sun
for the instant of their crossed paths.
*The European Union and the International Finance
Corporation have condemned Nigeria's execution...*

Chop. Thistles grown tough through a long summer
bend, and on the third strike, shred. *Saro-Wiwa,
President of the Organization for the Survival
of the Ogoni People, and eight other activists...*

Chop. Blisters come up. Blisters break. Sweat
in the eyes, sting in the palms, ache in the back.
*...arrested after protests against Shell Oil's destruction
of traditional lands in Nigeria's oil-rich southeast...*

Chop. A thud sickeningly wrong, and vision clears.
"No!" I am screaming at the back door of my
neighbor,
his bad luck to be lingering over coffee, a
veterinarian.

"Make it stop—" I shoved the blood-dripped mess
toward his chest, the rabbit's foreleg hanging
by a shred of furred skin, an intact tendon,
two fine, dis-jointed bones.

Even here the radio's blare echoes off the brick
of the patio's far wall. *...estimate that in 45 yearsthe*
world's remaining oil reserves will have been
exhausted...

"Make it stop." He closed his right hand
on the gaping wound, his left hand on my arm.
"It will be all right," he said.
"All bleeding stops
eventually."

PHOTO SHOOT

In grammar, the subject can never be the object. In a photography shoot, object is exactly what the subject is. "Let me come over and look in your closet. I'll pick out some things for you to wear. Do we need to bring a groomer, or do you do your own makeup and hair?" It's like letting someone play dolls with you.

"Sit there. Turn your head this way. Stand there. Come toward me a half step. Look right into my lens. Look over here at my fingers without moving your head. Beautiful; that's just beautiful." She said she loved my second-hand tweed jacket and my shawl-collared snowflake sweater. She said she loved my London Fog raincoat. "You're so tiny," she said. All my life I wanted to dress with style and to be thin.

I trusted her because she shot in black and white and wanted to shoot outdoors even though it was pouring rain. "I spotted some locations," she said, and showed me Polaroids—a picnic table in Avery Park, railroad tracks diverging at a switch, the Willamette pushing itself up against and past the concrete bridge supports of the Highway 34 bypass. There are nice scenes all over the place, okay settings, all right light. Sometimes there is one that is just true. "This," I said, pointing to the river. "We have to do this." I wanted to be the person framed against that swollen surge, my stagnant slough of a self overtaken by the winter flood. I wanted to belong to the river.

Next morning they arrived ten minutes late, without the Starbuck's coffee they had promised.

The assistants loaded me into the van with the equipment, said we could still stop for coffee, and drove straight to the first site. I was trying to be a good subject. I said, "We can get it later." We spent an hour at the park, the breaks in the rain blessed and the sun breaks cursed by the crew. Then we had an hour on the train tracks, curious town folk stopping to stare, a switch engine's hulk bearing down on us, lights flashing and horn clanging while she squeezed off "just two more."

Between shots, the cell phone beeped, the magazine's art editor demanding at the last minute that she shoot in color. "Impossible. I only use black and white. It's always in the contract. We use a very special film; you'll never find it. We're in this little tiny town, we're in the middle of nowhere, we're on the shoot for Christ sake, we only have another hour." "That crazy motherfucker. He's just jerking me around. Color is for tabloids. I never shoot color. It's the first question we ask when somebody calls the studio. Nobody in New York ever wants to work with this guy. He jerks people around like this all the time. They'll never find that film in color. Not around here. We can't even find it in New York." My neck had cramped from shivering. It had started to rain. We never went for coffee.

Finally, the river. I have been wandering for a long time, but this felt like home, here under the bridge, out of the rain but not the cold or the wind. For an hour, "Come closer. Step back. Profile." And to the assistants, "Bring me the Zeiss. Focus. More film. Let's do a Polaroid of that. Is her hair flaring against the sky? Open up. Close a half."

66

Even with two pairs of wool socks, Wellingtons were totally inadequate. My toes ached so with cold that I wished they would just hurry on to the next stage and become numb. I shivered and jumped around, flapped my arms and ran in place in between rolls of film. I faced the river and studied the wave and trough patterns where the flow met the abutments. When she shot, I stilled the chattering of my teeth by relaxing into the river's embrace at my back.

"Stretch," she said. "Raise up your arms as high as you can. More. Stretch." My bullshit detector was humming a low-level warning, not yet a full alert. What was this? It didn't feel like me. "More," she said, and my arms were out like Jesus crucified, and I knew for sure this was false. She must have noticed too because she backed off and said, "Profile. Now raise your arms."

I raised my arms and turned my face to the sky. I closed my eyes. And it took me over, that prayer of gratitude that would come upon me, always a surprise, all through the prison years, whenever I raised my face to the sun, the rain, the mist, the wind, the sleet, the stars against the blue-black sky, first faint honk of the low-flying geese. There by the river I was neither willing nor unwilling. Carried by my upturned face and upraised arms, gratitude prayed me, gratitude for cold-to-ice feet, for wind finding its way past my coat buttons down my neck, for the swollen river, for whatever I was doing putting myself into the hands of an artist.

She was on the last roll of film. We were finished. I had to be in school in half an hour. The assistants and the artist were muttering their relief that no one had shown up with the obscure color film when I spotted a skinny woman in a short leather coat heading for us from the parking lot. Mutterings turned to curses. She had no choice but to use the single roll.

"It's okay," I told her. "The river is brown and my coat is gray. It won't be a color picture anyway."

A NOTE FROM THE AUTHOR

Graceful survival, the work of prison days, is not separate from the searing introspection that is the work of prison years. I am deeply grateful for the individuals and institutions that penetrated the prison's permeable walls to bring life-giving beauty, joy, stimulation, and faith in my human possibility.

The work in these pages was made possible by two remarkable institutions. The Prison Education Program of Boston University's Metropolitan College is a passionate project of both the university and the professors who come to the prisons to teach. Their determination upholds the best traditions of the humanities, insisting that the life of the mind is an essential aspect of the human life, in all circumstances. They created the space and the structure where raw experience could be brought into language and crafted into poems and stories.

The College of Liberal Arts at Oregon State University injects the perspective of the humanities into a land and sea grant college, where work of the mind is grounded in challenges faced by an economy based on natural resources. I particularly want to acknowledge Kathleen Dean Moore of the Philosophy Department there for her help in unifying these works into a narrative whole.

CPSIA information can be obtained at www.ICGtesting.com
Printed in the USA
LVOW10s0042211113

362176LV00012BB/151/P